Somebody Needs to Hear What I Have to Say

Renita L. Smith

DEDICATION

I dedicate this book to the ancestors who have come before me and paved the way for me to become who I am today.

Contents

A Message to My Children

You think I'm being mean to you
That is not the truth
All I want is what's best for you
While you are going through.

Experience has taught me many things
I try to share each day
To help you avoid the road blocks
Standing in your way.

Listen to the wisdom
I give when you are wrong
Know I'll never hurt you
Just want to make you strong.

I'm sure you think I'm clueless
Of what may trouble you
But know that where you are today
I have been there too.

So, listen to the words I say
Even if you don't want to hear
 For one day the message I give to you
Might help to ease your fear.

Alone

You can't do it alone
You can't do it alone
Gotta wait till the Lord gets ready
You can't do it alone.

When your heart is heavy
And you are going through
Ask the Lord to help you
Let him see you through.

If you're lost and weary
Cannot find your way
Pray to God almighty
To help you through the day.

You can't do it alone
You can't do it alone
Gotta wait till the Lord gets ready
Because you can't do it alone.

American

Nigger, coon
Is that you
Definitely not me
I'm human too.

Slave, Servant
Is that you
No, I'm free
Just like you.

Colored, Negro
Is that you
Absolutely not
Those days are through.

Black, African American
Is that you
No, simply American
Just like you.

Angels

I wish that I could help you
But I don't know what to do
I will whisper a prayer
One made especially for you.

You will encounter trials
As you try and find your way
But know that God is with you
Each and every day.

You have been sent an angel
To help you through your pain
So just be patient in knowing
Sunshine will follow the rain.

Appreciate

You don't appreciate feeling good
Until you start feeling bad
You don't appreciate being happy
Until you start being sad.

You don't appreciate joy
Until you feel the pain
You don't appreciate sunshine
Until you see the rain.

You can't appreciate good health
Until you become ill
You can't overcome adversity
Unless it's in God's will.

Because I Am Human

Because I am human
I cannot know what tomorrow will bring.
Because I am human
I cannot know what God has in store for me.
Because I am human
My faith gets weak, I am tested.
Because I am human
I must have faith that God will see me through this thing
That I... on my own cannot comprehend and figure out.
Because I am human
I must trust God with all my might.
Because I am human, a child of God
I must know that
Because I am human
All things will work out for the good for all of those who
love and serve the Lord.
Because I AM HUMAN
I pray, wait, be patient, and know that all is well.

Black and Invisible

Stop looking over me
For I am not invisible
See the greatness that stands before you
Give me a chance to succeed.

Stop looking over me
For I am not invisible
Engage me and discover
How gifted I really am.

Stop looking over me
For I am not invisible
Allow intelligence to meet opportunity
And accept that I am black, but not invisible.

Childhood

Take me back to my childhood
So that I can again be free
Allow me to get away
From the things that puzzle me.

Take me back to the days
Where there are no worries there
Flowing effortlessly through life
Just did not have a care.

Take me to the river
Where the cool waters flow
Effortlessly traveling through
Not worrying where to go.

Take me to the mountaintop
Where I'll be nearer to him
A place where there is peace
Away from a world so dim.

Take me to a peaceful place
Where I will worry no more
A place of pure perfection
Away from the world I know.

Take me to a place on earth
Where living is just a breeze
Where every challenge we encounter
Will be mastered with effortless ease.

Take me to my childhood
Where trouble will be no more
Every day will be blissful peace
Today and forever more.

Communication

Communication
The foundation
Of all we say and do.

If you fail to talk to me
How do you expect me
To understand you.

Communicating is a simple thing
Many try to avoid
When you fail to talk to me
We're left with such a void.

Find a way to communicate
If you want to have peace
When you choose to communicate
All conflict will then cease.

Crying

Come to me as humble as you know how

Release all your sorrows

Yearn to be closer to me, for I am the way

Invite me into your heart so that I may ease your pain

Never cease praying

Give God all your troubles and leave them there.

Dream Killer

Stop killing the dreams
I have within
The goals I've set for self.

These are dreams
Designed for me
Reserved for no one else.

Encourage me to be my best
Help me along the way
Stop killing the dreams
I have within
To be somebody someday.

If your goal is to kill my dream
Stay far, far away
Let me move to reach my goal
To find success my way.

Don't kill the dream!

Drunk Man

What makes a drunk man drink
Drowning in his sorrows
Too afraid to think
Drinking his pain away
Forgetting about tomorrow.

What makes a drunk man drink
To pass the time away
Bring relief to hurt inside
Make it through another day.

What makes a drunk man drink
Yesterday, today, tomorrow
Joy, pain, a heavy heart
Simply so he does not have to think.

Easy Ain't Easy

Easy isn't always easy
When you're going through
This thing that's called easy
Can be complicated too.

Easy is not easy
You think it is a breeze
Easy isn't always easy
Can put you on bended knees.

If you think it's easy
Working simple out
One day you will discover
Easy can be hard without a doubt.

Easy just ain't easy!

Education in America

Education in America
Is not on solid ground
The current system is broken
A solution must be found.

All learners are not equal
The way they're taught today
The ones who have the money
Have a better way.

Economics determines
The knowledge children acquire
If you have no money
Your future is quite dire.

We have the power to change it
Equality is a must
Let's change the course of education
A must for all of us.

Embrace Knowledge

Embrace knowledge
While you can
For this knowledge
Waits on no man.

Knowledge is powerful
Don't you know
Knowledge will help you
Wherever you go.

Make it your business
Get all that you can
Some for yourself
And your fellow man.

The more you know
The easier it will be
For you to become
Who you want to be.

Embrace knowledge
While you can
A sound investment
Worth $$$ in the hand.

Forgiveness #1

Something happened
The moment you asked
Asked for forgiveness.

I felt something
Unexplainable
A feeling deep down inside.

The power of forgiveness
Opens doors
One never knew existed.

Something happened
The moment you asked
Asked to be forgiven.

I did and now I am free.

Forgiveness #2

Forgiveness is a very
Difficult thing to do
Forgiveness is not for them
Forgiveness is for you.

No matter what the issue
You must let it go
You must forgive the matter
So that you can grow.

If you want forgiveness
For the things you do
You must forgive others
And God will forgive you too.

When someone has wronged you
Don't go around mad or sad
Find your way to forgiveness
Some day you will be glad.

Friends

True Friends...

Give more than they take
Share more than they keep
Love more than they hate
Console when you weep
Don't judge when you are wrong
Yet help you to stay strong.

Real friends

PRICELESS!

Genocide by Design

A black man is born
His future is bleak
He strives for greatness
But his will is weak.

A system designed
To keep him off track
Designer clothes, cars, fast money,
and CRACK.

Integration didn't help his cause
The education system
Put his genius on pause.

Who does he look up to, you say
A fictitious symbol
To show him the way.

Whoa! We're losing our children
That's a fact
It is our time
To take them back.

Before they
Destroy their minds
Let us stop this

GENOCIDE BY DESIGN!

God is Good

God is good
God is great
What he does
Is never too late.

Steps right in
Right on time
Takes good care
Of these needs of mine.

I don't worry
I don't fret
God almighty
Hasn't failed me yet.

God Will Feed Your Purpose

God will feed your purpose
The job he's given to you
If you follow instructions
He'll give you guidance too.

Your purpose is for others
Not to make you grand
Follow the purpose before you
It's for your fellow man.

Don't look for fame or fortune
As you complete your task
God has already blessed you
Even before you asked.

Go on and stay on purpose
Do what you're called to do
He'll pour you out a blessing
To always carry you through.

Going Through

Right now, I'm going through something
I don't know what to do
As I seek the answer
I pause and pray to you.

Yes, my heart is heavy
Why, I do not know
Life will bring me trials
But God sits high and looks low.

I put my trust in Jesus
For he will see me through
I'll always pray and keep the faith
That he'll do what he promised to do.

Gotta Go Through It

You gotta go through it
Before you get to it
That's the way it goes
The journey won't seem easy
Will keep you on your toes.

You gotta go through it
Before you get to it
The road feels long and rough
Just keep your mind on Jesus
He'll bring you through all the stuff.

You gotta go through it
Before you get to it
Be patient along the way
One foot in front of the other
Just take it day by day.

You gotta go through it
Before you get to it
Although the wait is hard
Put your trust in Jesus
And do what says the Lord.

Now you have gone through it
And you have gotten to it
Peace is in your heart
When you depend on Jesus
The trials are not so hard.

You gotta go through it
Before you get to it
Whatever your it happens to be
Get started on your journey
To reach your destiny.

Go through it
Get to it
Just do it!

Greed

I'm not one to be greedy
All I need is enough
Just a small amount of money
To pay for this worldly stuff.

I'm not one to be greedy
Giving back is part of the plan
Just a small amount of money
To help my fellow man.

I'm not one to be greedy
Saving for a rainy day
Just a small amount of money
To help me along the way.

I'm not trying to be greedy
Working by day and night
Just a small amount of money
With that I will be alright.

Hate

Hate is a very strong word to use
Sometimes it's just how I feel
Don't use the word toward people
Just situations, I'm keeping it real.

I hate the way some things are
The way they turn out to be
Just so very disgusted
Hatred won't flee from me.

I try so much to avoid it
The things that get me down
Every time I look around
Despair is easily found.

Hate is a very strong word to use
Pray about it come what may
Hatred will soon be put to rest
Looking forward to that day.

Head vs. Heart

Live from your heart
Not from your head
Your heart won't lead you astray.

Living from your head
And not from your heart
May cause trouble along the way.

Heart is where your spirit resides
With guidance to carry you through
Listen to instructions
It constantly gives to you.

Help is there when you need it
You just need to ask
Then wait for your directions
To help you with your task.

You are never alone
Your heart is always there
Eager to assist you
It does not matter where.

So, when you need assistance
Problems big and small
Live from your heart
Not from your head
And know you will not fall.

Heaven on Earth

There is a place called heaven
I've been told I want to go
If there is a heaven
For sure I do not know.

I believe this place exists
Where life will just be grand
But give me a little peace
Down here with my fellow man.

Heaven in heaven, wonderful
Heaven on earth should be too
Just want to have equality
And enjoy all things like you.

So, let me have some heaven
Down here in this old place
Then when this life is done down here
I'll be finished with this race.

His

I am a child of God
Working hard to do his will
I am a child of God
His love for me is real.

I am a child of God
Perfection is my goal
I am a child of God
Striving to be made whole.

I am a child of god
Loving him with all my heart
I am a child of God
Our love will never part.

I Am...

Loved
Covered by the precious blood of God
Protected
A Child of God
God's gift to the world.

I Am One

I am one, the only one
That God has chosen for this journey
Alone I can and will do great things
The struggle is so real that it is unreal.

I am one, the only one
Who can fight this battle
The fight is not an easy one
But it can and will be conquered.

I am one, the only one
Who will succeed in this journey that I am on

I am one, the only one.

I Give Thanks

Thank you, God
For another day
For ordering my steps
And showing me the way.

Thank you, Lord
For keeping me wise
From making bad decisions
That may lead to my demise.

Thank you, Lord
For walking by my side
For drying all the tears
That I have ever cried.

I Quit My Job

The only thing that I can fix
Without a doubt is me
Since you did not want me
I chose to set me free.

I tried to work within your means
You would not let it be
So, I chose to make a change
And let myself be free.

My conscious mind wanted to stay
To hold on to what is familiar
Did all I could to make it work
The end was getting nearer.

The only thing that I can change
My words, deeds, and actions
When I chose to take that step
I found such great satisfaction.

This old place no longer for me
This thing that's known as work
What I now have come to know
This job was not a perk.

Now that I have set me free
Feel better than ever before
From this day I will move on
My peace has been restored.

The moral of this writing is
Money doesn't always give relief
Sometimes you must make a change
Before you find true peace.

If it is Me

Lord, Lord, if it is me
Open my eyes that I may see
Lord, Lord, if it is me
Help me to become the best I can be.

Show me how to walk in the light
Help me to strive to do what is right
As I travel this path each day
Lead me and guide me to the right way.

When I am lost, traveling the wrong road
Take all my burdens and lighten my heavy load
Give me the wisdom to stay in your will
To wait for your voice just sit and be still.

In all the things that I say and do
Let them Lord be pleasing to you
Keep the faith and trust in your word
For with God almighty my prayers will be heard.

I'm More Than My Body

I am more than my body
I have a heart, a mind, a soul
I am more than my body.

My heart needs protecting
My mind needs stimulating
My soul needs nurturing.

I am more than my body
I am a woman
Respect me for being
God's gift to you.

For I am
More than my Body.

I'm More Than That

Talk about me
As much as you please
I know just who I am
I'll never let those words you speak
Put me in a jam.

The mean old things
You say about me
Words that don't hold true
I'll walk and hold my head up high
Won't give my power to you.

So, go ahead and talk about me
Your words just make me strong
I'll be the person I'm destined to be
And prove your words to be wrong.

It's Not About Me

It's not about me
Can't you see
I'm striving to do
The work God's given to me.

As I travel
Come what may
Helping my fellow man
See a brighter day.

It's not about me
Because I must do
What God has told me
To do for you.

It's not about me
Even though things get hard
Have to keep on doing
What's spoken by the Lord.

It's not about me
The pains I endure
I'll get my blessing
Of that I am sure.

So, keep on toiling
Come what may
Know that God
Will lead the way.

**Keep on trusting
In the word
For sure I'll get
What I deserve.**

It's What I Feel

It's what I feel
The words I speak
I will not hide
I am not weak.

Whatever comes
Into my heart
I'll say aloud
From finish to start.

Don't silence me
I must proclaim
These truthful words
In Jesus name.

So, from now on
I vow to say
What comes to mind
In my own way.

Jesus Loves You

Jesus loves you
And so do I
There is no special reason why.

You will always have
A special place in my heart
The love I have for you
Will never depart.

No matter what
The future may be
Just always know
You mean the world to me.

I will be forever grateful
For all the things you do
A smile, a deed, or just a word
To help me make it through.

God has truly blessed me
Allowing you in my life
Thanks for being the person you are
And truly enriching my life.

Just Have to Wait

When life is not going
The way you think it should
And you can't see around the corner
You just have to wait.

When you ask for a blessing
You think you want need or deserve
You just have to wait.

When you don't get the job
You feel you deserve
You just have to wait.

When money doesn't come your way
When you think it should
You just have to wait.

When the one you think you love
Loves someone else
You just have to wait.

When things just don't seem
To be happening for you
You just have to wait.

When you tell your truth
Hoping others will listen and believe
You just have to wait.

Wait for things to work out
As they should
Waiting is hard.

Because you cannot see your way
Your blessing is around the corner
But you just have to wait.

Just Look Up

When you are down
And feeling low
So confused
Not knowing where to go
JUST LOOK UP!

When life is hard
And friends are few
So discouraged
Don't know what to do
JUST LOOK UP!

When you're alone
Can't see your way
Hoping to see
A brighter day
JUST LOOK UP!

When you're in doubt
About any little thing
Confused about
What the future will bring

JUST LOOK UP!

Knowledge

Embrace knowledge
While you can
For this knowledge
Waits on no man.

Knowledge is powerful
Don't you know
Knowledge will help you
Wherever you go.

Make it your business
Get all that you can
Some for yourself
And some for your fellow man.

The more you know
The easier it will be
For you to become
Who you want to be.

Embrace knowledge
While you can
As sound investment
Worth money in the hand.

Knowledge, Wisdom, Understanding

Get knowledge, wisdom, and understanding
Each and every day
If you take them with you
God will show you the way.

Knowledge is a powerful weapon
To help you make it through
You'll make the best decisions
From knowledge God gives to you.

Wisdom, don't go without it
Be wise and don't despair
With wisdom you can make it
Here there and everywhere.

God gives you understanding
Proverbs tells you so
Study to understand it
Take it everywhere you go.

Knowledge, wisdom, understanding
Gifts given by God
If you use them wisely
Your trials will not be hard.

Labels

Stop putting
A label on me
I am who I am
Can't you see?

Just because
I am not you
Doesn't mean I'm unable
To do the things you do.

I am unique
In my own way
I can succeed
If you let me have my say.

I may not do things
The way you want me to
Does not mean
That I don't know how to.

If you will allow me
I promise this to you
I will succeed
In what I choose to do.

Life Ain't Right

Life ain't right
Life ain't fair
So much deception
Everywhere.

People caring
Only for self
Refusing to help
Someone else.

Life ain't right
Life ain't fair
So much hatred
Here and there.

Until we make
A drastic change
Everything will
Stay the same.

Life ain't right
Life ain't fair
I pray someday
We'll start to care.

Little Bird

Ever watch a little bird fly
Moving ever so freely through the sky
Ever listen to the little bird sing
Singing and not worrying about a thing?

Ever see the bird build a sturdy nest
Taking care of home not concerned about the rest
Ever notice her care for the young
Making preparation for the days to come?

Why can't we be like the little bitty bird
Minding our own business without saying a word
Why can't we sing a heavenly song
While making our blessed house a home?

If we could only mimic the bird we see
You and I could be free, free, free
So, take a lesson from our friend in the sky
Work hard and be happy
Find peace by and by.

Living

Living simply or simply living
Which one applies to you
Are you living simply
Or simply making it through?

When you're living simply
You are within your means
But if you are simply living
You're going to the extreme.

Be cautious of simply living
An extravagant way of life
Embrace living simply
Avoid unnecessary strife.

Now you know the difference
Which one do you choose
Will you be living simply
Or is simply living for you?

Love

People learn how to love
From the images they see
That image could be you
And it could be me.

Give full attention
To all the things you do
Because you never know
Who is watching you.

Just be full aware
Of the power you possess
One wrong decision
Could cause someone to regress.

Every person has
The power deep within
To shine a positive light
Brightly before all men.

As you go about
Your duties for this day
Teach someone to love
In a very positive way.

People learn how to love
From the images that they see
That image could be you
And that image could be me.

Love is What Love Is

Love is what love is
You can't force it
You can't change it.

Love is what love is
You can't choose it
It chooses you unexpectedly.

Love is what love is
A gift from God above
You cannot hide it, for it is real.

Love is what love is
The strongest addiction
It cannot be overcome.

Love is what love is
It lies deep within
A common emotion we all share.

Love is what love is
You can't avoid it
For it will surely come.

Love is what love is
Accept it
Endure it.

Love is what love is
Believe it
Receive
Because love is what love is.

Many Nights

Many nights crying
Many days sighing
Don't know what to do.

Keep on trusting
Keep on praying
That God will see me through.

Up all night
Could not sleep
Afraid to close my eyes.

Did not know
What the moment would bring
Had to keep my eyes on the prize.

Day by day
Had to hold on
To my undying faith.

Knowing that
The God I serve
Will somehow make a way.

Me

I am different, I am me
God made me special, uniquely
He gave me eyes, so I could see
He gave me a mind to be
The best I can be.

I am special I am me
I will achieve
Just wait and see.

Missed

Oh, how I miss you
You taught me so much
Living, loving, laughing
The gentleness of your touch.

Oh, how I miss you
Lessons held deep within
All the things you taught me
I long to see you again.

Although you're gone to heaven
I think of you every day
When I need direction
I think of the words you would say.

Yes, I miss you dearly
I know I must go on
I'll see you someday in heaven
Meanwhile, I'll just press on.

Mother

There is no other
Like a good mother
A gift from God above
In everything she does and says
Always showing her love.

Mothers are very special
Always go out of the way
Working hard and doing her best
To give you a brighter day.

There is no other
Like a good mother
She deserves the ultimate respect
As she approaches the golden years
Be sure you don't neglect.

Be grateful for the mom you have
The only one you will get
Take care of her while you can
So you won't have regrets.

On this day I honor you
Best mom that one could have
I'll always be grateful for
Good times that we have shared.

My Sister in Christ

To my sister in Christ
Thank you for being you
For so many days
Your words help me get through.

God has truly blessed me
He put you in my path
The simple things you do and say
What better blessing to have.

To my beautiful sister
I'm grateful for all you do
I pray that God will bless you
As you are going through.

Thank you for the blessing
You give to me each day
A deed, a smile, a simple word
Helps me along the way.

To you my sister in Christ
Thanks for being you
For all the simple things you do
To help me make it through.

Nature

What makes…

sun rise
oceans tide
trees grow
rivers flow
skies blue
rainbow hue
earth round
thunder sound
clouds rain
seasons change
flowers bloom
full moon
cool breeze
winter freeze
fierce storm
tornadoes form
clouds gray
gloomy day

Nature

Never too Late

It's never too late
For you to do
The thing that brings
Most joy to you.

Make up your mind
And then commit
Work toward your goal
Bit by bit.

Follow the path
Laid out for you
Do not stop trying
Until you are through.

Plant enough seeds
Something is bound to grow
If it's worthy
I'm sure you will know.

It's never too late
You're never too old
Step out be great
Don't put it on hold.

It's never too late.

Nothing but a Feeling

Sex
Nothing but a feeling
Gone in an instant
Love is everlasting.

Sex
Nothing but a feeling
Momentous
Love is everlasting.

Sex
Nothing but a feeling
Fleeing in the night
Love is everlasting.

Sex
Nothing but a feeling
Gone too soon
Love is everlasting.

Sex

Ain't nothing but a feeling.

On Bended Knees

A heavy heart
A soul is weak
Guidance Lord
Is what I seek.

Weary Lord
Can't find my way
Lost all power
So now I pray.

I'll be still and silent too
Then kneel down
And wait for you.

On bended knees
I will pray
The Holy Spirit
Will lead the way.

From now on
Let come what may
On bended knees
I'll kneel and pray.

One Day

One day my heart was heavy
Then I began to sigh
I called upon Lord Jesus
To ask him Lord, Lord why?

And when I spoke to Jesus
He answered right away
A voice appeared and said to me
Don't sigh my child just pray.

I followed God's instructions
Fell on my knees that day
I asked the Lord to help me please
Teach me how to pray.

Our father who art in heaven
Is how you must begin
Hallowed be thy holy name
Just let the words sink in.

Thy kingdom come thy will be done
On earth as it is in heaven
Give us this day our daily bread
Forgive us as we forgive our debtors.

And lead us not into temptation
Is what you now must say
But deliver us from evil
As we travel along the way.

For thine is the kingdom
As we work to make it in
The power and glory forever

And now just say AMEN.

Power Tripping

No man on earth is perfect
We're all created the same
Just because you lead me
Doesn't put you ahead of the game.

We all have special gifts
Given to us by God
We all must work together
Everyone must do their part.

You call yourself a leader
Charged to show us the way
But don't let your position
Let you go astray.

Stop your power tripping
Let's get on one accord
Work hand and hand together
And do what thus says the Lord.

You are not any better
Than those of us you lead
Stop your power tripping
Respect the one's you need.

One last thing I must tell you
As I go my way
Stop your power tripping
Do it right away.

Prayer

Lord, I thank you
For bringing me through
All the trying times
I didn't know what to do.

Thank you for the blessings
Given to me each day
Thank you for all the times
You helped me find my way.

Lord, I thank you
For all the things you give
Allowing me to have
Another day to live.

Thank you for the goodness
That's been given to me
For I truly know
You didn't have to let it be.

Lord, I just thank you
For everything you do
For waking me up this morning
To start this day anew.

Reason, Season, Lifetime

<u>A Reason</u>: Why you are doing the thing God has assigned you to do.

<u>A Season</u>: The appointed time you are given to complete the task.

<u>A Lifetime</u>: Those things that endure the test of time and will never leave you.

It can be a friend, a job, a family member, a memory, etc.

Reflect on your reasons

Understand and know the season

Treasure the lifetimes

Retirement

I've paid my dues
Time to be through
I'm about to pass
The torch on to you.

I've done my best
The best that I could
I've given my all
As anyone should.

Now it's time
To take my rest
And let someone else
Take over this mess.

I'm done!

Saggin

To those fine brothers of mine
Why must you wear those pants on your behind?

So, you think you are hip and cool
Oh no my brother you just look like a fool.

Why do you think you are treated so bad
Could it be that you are a slave to fad?

Don't fall prey to everything that comes along
For it's only a means of keeping you off the throne.

Oh, my brother you were born of a Queen
So, arise my brother and be a King of Kings.

Don't let the saggin' keep you behind
Rise my brother and be the pride of all mankind.

Use your unique genius God has given you today
Chart a path of greatness for those along the way.

Put an end to saggin', let's leave it behind
Go forth and do great things
For the good of all mankind.

Secrets

Ladies, Ladies
Too much breast
Be more cautious
Of the way you dress.

Pants too tight, hair so fly
Men mistreat you
And you wonder why.

Check yourself, tone it down
Then carry yourself like
The jewels in a crown.

Be more careful
Of the words you say
Those mean old words
May be your truth someday.

Are you beautiful
Oh, without a doubt
Dare to be subtle
Then let them check you out.

Don't create attention
Just to be seen
Let your inner self
Make you a beauty queen.

From this day forward
When you step out
Stop, look and think
Don't let your secrets out.

Small Talk

People will say
What they want to say
What matters is how you take it
Hold your head up anyway
And know you're going to make it.

Don't let those silly words they speak
Bring your spirit down
Because you know just who you are
You will make it round by round.

Something

Everybody goes through something
It's just not in print
The good, the bad, the ugly
Of how our lives are spent.

Some things are kept secret
Others not so much
The way we choose to live our lives
Can put us in a rut.

Everybody goes through something
Difficult it may be
Put your trust in Jesus
Let you soul be free.

When you go through something
Thinking you're all alone
Ask the Lord for guidance
Let him make you strong.

Everybody goes through something
No one is exempt
Lean not to your understanding
Rely completely on him.

Everybody goes through something.

Sometimes

Sometimes you just gotta let it go
Sometime the tears just have to flow
Sometimes the pain, the pain just gets so hard
Find comfort in knowing
That God is never far.

Sometimes you wonder
Why it is me
Going through these changes
Thinking how can this be?

Sometimes you think
You got it all figured out
Only to realize
You must turn about.

Sometimes you simply think
I'll quit, I just can't win
That's the very moment
When God just steps right in.

So, when you sometimes feel
That you cannot go on
Always remember
That God is on the throne.

Strength

These days have been an adventure
A roller coaster ride
Up today down tomorrow
But I stayed right by your side.

You have shown me strength
That's beyond compare
But now your soul is weary
With your crosses to bear.

You wanted me to leave you
That I could not do
My heart just would not let me
I had to see you through.

Yes, my heart is heavy
As you prepare to make it in
But I can rest in knowing
This race you're sure to win.

I pray to my Heavenly Father
I hope that I can be
A fraction of the person
You have lived to be.

I'm proud to call you mother
As proud as one can be
Take your rest in knowing
Your soul can now be free.

Subliminal Messages

Subliminal Messages
Are dangerous you see
Designed to influence
Both you and me.

Subliminal messages
Are everywhere
In all places
Both here and there.

Be very cautious
Of what you see and hear
For their messages
Are always very near.

Subliminal messages
Cause you to react
To make poor choices
Without all the facts.

Subliminal messages
Ain't no joke
Watch out they can cause
You to go broke.

Teacher

I listened to the rest
But I was taught by the best
Let no man control you mind
Leave those subliminal messages behind.

I listened to the rest
But I was taught by the best.
Let no man determine your fate
Follow you heart if you want to be great.

I listened to the rest
But I was taught by the best
For all your needs look deep within
Follow the spirit you're sure to win.

I listened to the rest
But I was taught by the best
Follow your heart in all that you do
Know that I will see you through.

Tears

All cried out
No tears to shed
Only God knows
What lies ahead.

No more sickness
No more pain
Rest in peace
Great memories remain.

Time ain't long
It's winding down
One day soon
You'll wear your crown.

On your way
To your home on high
Just rest in knowing
It's never goodbye.

So, farewell
For a short time
We'll meet again
In the sweet by and by.

Teen

To my beautiful sister
I know being a teen is hard
But keep your self-composure
And finish the things you start.

They'll say mean things about you
Those things you can't control
Stand tall and stay on purpose
And faith will see you through.

Remember you have a purpose
On this earth today
Don't listen to the mean old words
The other people say.

You are born for greatness
Don't give your power away
Be better than those who mock you
And find success today.

Your peers will give you pressure
To help you go astray
Be strong and follow the lessons
You have been taught today.

Young men will tell you sweet things
They think you want to hear
Listen very closely
Be sure they are sincere.

To my beautiful sister
I know being a teen is hard
But know the choice is yours to make
Stop, think, and follow your heart.

Ten Days to Live

If I had ten days to live
Here is what I'd truly give
I'd give my love to all I meet
And give the hungry food to eat.

If I had 9 days to go
Unselfishness is what I'd show
For all of those who may have less
I'd use my gifts, so they'd be blessed.

If I had just 8 more days
I'd work to avoid the evil ways
I'd pray and ask dear God above
To show me how to always love.

If I had only 7 days left
Before I draw my very last breath
I'd do my best to avoid sin
On my quest to make it in.

If I had just 6 days more
I'd sing God's praises forevermore
I'd sing heavenly songs to God on high
On my way to heaven in the sky.

If I had 5 days to pray
I'd ask the Father just what to say
Now I know which words to use
I'd use the words to spread the good news.

If I had 4 days to be
The Christian God would like to see
I'd walk in light and follow God's word
I'd make sure God's message is heard.

If I had just 3 days to
Do the things that are best for you
I'd introduce you to God above
For you to experience his undying love.

If I had 2 days of life
I'd teach you how to avoid strife
I'd show you how to study the word
And let your Godly voice be heard.

Now I have just 1 more day
I'll praise my Father all the way
I'll pray to the Lord on my way in
To please forgive me of all my sins.

Yes, my time on earth is done
And the earthly race is won
I'll look down from heaven above
And hope those left will
Share God's love.

The Flag

When the flag was created
We were not all free
The flag was not designed
Or created for me.

The flag is a symbol
Of things that have been done
It does not signify
That my race has won.

Stand up salute and honor it you say
The symbol does not move me
Doesn't move me in any way.

Do I love this country?
For the most part, yes, I do
I just simply choose not to honor the flag
The same way that you do.

Do not dwell in anger
Because I disagree
The flag, the symbol that you love
Doesn't mean the same to me.

The flag is an innate object
Not designed to be praised
I save the praises that I have
For God above every day.

The Gift of Gab

The gift of gab
I do not have
Talking is not my thing
I'd rather use the written word
To let my voice be seen.

The gift of gab
I do not have
Spoken words aren't easy for me
I'd rather use the written word
For everyone to see.

I am grateful for
The gift I have
To use my words this way
Even without the gift of gab
My voice is heard anyway.

I promise to use
The gift I have
To help someone along the way
And hope the written words I choose
Will brighten up your day.

The Man

When you're working for the man
No time to just do you
All tied up and tangled up
You don't know what to do.

When you're working for the man
Your thoughts are not your own
All you do is spend your time
Working fingers to the bone.

Always working for the man
Content is not your mind
Now it's time to flip the script
And do your thing this time.

No longer do you work for him
Your mind is now at peace
Take the time to meditate
Be who you want to be.

Find the thing that gives you joy
Like nothing has before
Then and only then you'll find
Your work is now your toy.

The Mirror

When you look in the mirror
As you often do
Do you like the image
Staring back at you?

When you look in the mirror
Red, black, white, yellow, tan
Do you ever think about
How you treat your fellow man?

Look again in the mirror
Who's looking back at you
Remember the image you're seeing
Is the image that God sees too.

One more look in the mirror
Look closely at every part
Don't dwell on outer beauty
Because God looks at your heart.

The mirror has a message
For you on this day
If you do not like it
Change it right away.

The mirror will always show you
Nothing but the truth
What you do with the message
Is totally up to you.

If you choose to change it
Let it be for the best
Pray and ask for guidance
Let God take care of the rest.

The Right to Wear White

The right to wear white
Oh, what a sight
To see the ones who sit
Unfortunately, the ones that's there
Are not always legit.

Wearing white in America
A means to separate
Great big I's and little old u's
Can never make us great.

In the dear old USA
Today in such a mess
If we keep this nonsense up
No doubt we will regress.

There is no justice in this place
All are not treated fair
Those who are the ones who lead
Won't let us have our share.

Looking back over the years
Nothing has really changed
If you are a minority
Your plight is just the same.

Back at this old place again
Just in a different role
Unable to make some progress
Still in the same old hole.

Ashamed to say this is my world
Doesn't help my people at all
People slipping through the cracks
Eventually they just fall.

I pray the plight of this old place
Will change its wicked ways
Become a place for all to reap
Justice every day.

The White House

A black man in the White House
A house that's built by slaves
Who would have thought
He'd be running it someday.

A black man in the White House
Standing proud and tall
A beauty by his side
She won't let him fall.

A black man in the White House
One term, oh no but two
Always working tirelessly
To make life better for you.

Thoughts

Thought about something
Couldn't help but smile
What I thought about
Haven't done in a while.

Thought about something
Just how it made me feel
Just simply knowing
Your love for me is real.

Thought about something
To help me along the way
Giving me the strength
To make it through each day.

Thought about something
To always carry me through
Knowing you will always love me
And I will love you too.

Tired

I'm tired
I want to give up
Gotta keep going
Although the road is rough.

I'm tired
I want to sit down
Gotta keep going
I want to get my crown.

I'm tired
No longer want to try
Have to keep on laughing
Otherwise I'll simply cry.

I'm tired
Want to make it right
Have to keep on toiling
If I'm going to see the light.

I am tired
I refuse to give in
I'll keep pushing forward
That's the only way I can win.

To Stella

In the words of my dear Stella
She'd say without a frown
To all the young ladies
Drawers up and dresses down.

Stella had a message
To all who came and sat
Change your evil ways or be
Jail bait and penitentiary rats.

Stella gave us wisdom
In the most unusual way
I carry those wise words with me
Day -by -day -by -day.

I'm grateful to my dear Stella
For all the things she said
She planted the seed within me
To put knowledge in my head.

Trust

Get quiet
Get clear
Knowing that
God is near.

Open your eyes
Open your heart
He will guide you
From finish to start.

Do not rush
Because he loves you
Just that much.

Do not fret
Don't despair
You'll be covered
Everywhere.

Undercover Lover

I will not be
Your undercover lover
If you step to me
There cannot be another.

I choose not to be
Your undercover lover
The only place for me
Above all the others.

An undercover lover
A secret in the dark
Never is allowed
On daylight to embark.

I refuse to be
Your undercover lover
That is no place for me
As an undercover lover.

What Do You See

What do you see
When you see me?

Do you see beauty
Do you see character
Do you see intelligence?

What do you see
When you see me?

Do you look beyond the surface
Do you look to see who I really am?

What do you see
When you see me?

What You Gonna Do

Youngster, Youngster
What you gonna do
When you don't graduate
No one will hire you?

Out there looking
No job in site
Looking back and thinking
Should' studied with all my might.

Youngster, Youngster
What you gonna do
Ain't got no money
All your bills are due?

Now it's time to get up
Turn your life around
Get to the place
Where knowledge can be found.

Youngster, youngster
What you gonna do
Stay in school and graduate
Best thing for you to do.

Where is He

Where is God when you need him
Right there by your side
Wiped every tear away
Every time you cried.

There for your protection
Everywhere you go
He won't leave or forsake you
This you need to know.

God is your provider
For your every need
Just simply trust him
Your soul he's sure to feed.

God is an awesome God
This the world should know
Open your heart and let him in
Everywhere you go.

Who Am I

Who am I?
I am proud strong and gifted
I Am a Black man in Christ.

Who am I?
I am proud strong and gifted
I am a Black woman in Christ.

Who am I?
I am also proud strong and gifted but haven't reached my potential yet
I am a Black child in Christ.

Who am I?
I am one who has been bought with the precious blood of the most High King
And now I am adopted into his family.

Who am I?
I Am now of Royal blood with a rich heritage that's beyond all measure and imagination.

Who Am I?
I am that he says I Am
I am a simply a Child of God
And no one can ever take that away from me.

Who Are We

Who are we as a people
If we don't change a thing
Who are we as a people
If we won't let freedom ring?

Who are we as a people
If our past is still our present
Who are we as a people
If our lives aren't any better?

When we read our history
Of things done yesterday
We see there is no mystery
We are doing things the same old way.

Who are we as a people
If we fail to change anything
Who are we as a people
If we don't let freedom ring?

Wisdom

Older, grayer, wiser
Longevity has its place
Listen to your elders
As you run this race.

Lessons learned from elders
Who have gone before
Will always be there for you
Today and evermore.

Don't take those lessons lightly
If they don't make sense today
Soon they will come in handy
When you find you're going astray.

Yes, they are older and wiser
There's a reason for these things
To pass along the wisdom
And help you reach your dream.

Words

Words, words
Such powerful words
I must put them out there
Because I need to be heard.

Beautiful thoughts
Lying deep within
Not good at speaking
Therefore, I use my pen.

Writing is my voice
For all of you to see
I can't say it like you
So, I write it like me.

Words, words
Such powerful words
I can, I must write
So I can be heard.

I have so many messages
Lying deep within
What shall I do
I must share them
With my pen.

Work

Do what God
Put you here to do
Keep on working
Till he says you're through.

Though your job
Will often seem hard
Keep on working
Toward your reward.

Keep on striving
To reach your goal
Knowing that
He will make you whole.

As you travel
Day by day
Stay on task
Come what may.

God is watching
Your every move
So, do your best
To follow the rules.

If you work
And follow God's plan
You have no need
To fear any man.

God has promised
If you keep him first
He will surely
Quench your very thirst.

So, on your way
While you're going through
Do not fail to do
What God put you here to do.

Why

Why do the odds often seem stacked against me

When all I really want is to live and be free?

Free from all the external pressures in life

That causes each day to be so full of strife.

Why must I struggle so hard to achieve

What everyone knows is prevented by greed?

Greed that comes from the ones in control

They continuously study how to keep us on hold.

Why must it all be about black or white

Why must the black man continue to fight?

Fight for his dignity fight for his pride

Sometimes choosing to simply run and hide.

My only solace really comes when I pray

Pray that my father will show me the way.

Should this plight continue to trouble my race

I must I can I will overcome the trials of this evil place.

Yesterday

Yesterday God told me
Every thing's going to be alright
Put one foot before the other
Don't give up the fight.

Though you may be weary
And often want to fret
One thing to always remember
He has not failed you yet.

Continue on your journey
As you are going through
Have faith in knowing
God is there with you.

When God gives a message
Be sure to take it in
Simply follow his directions
He will be with you until the end.

Somebody Needs to Hear What I Have to Say

www.ingramcontent.com/pod-product-compliance
Lightning Source LLC
Chambersburg PA
CBHW070519030426
42337CB00016B/2024